The Purpose Driven Life

THE WORKBOOK

Disclaimer:

This workbook is for informational and educational purposes only, based on the author's teachings of life's purpose and spirituality. It is not a substitute for professional spiritual guidance, and individual interpretations may vary. Readers assume responsibility for their spiritual journey, and the author/publisher are not liable for any outcomes. Seek guidance from trusted sources to enrich your understanding of life's meaning.

LESSONS IN THIS WORKBOOK:

1. It All Starts with God

2. You Are Not an Accident

3. What Drives Your Life?

4. Made to Last Forever

5. Seeing Life from God's View

6. Life Is a Temporary Assignment

7. The Reason for Everything

Chapter 1:
It All Starts with God

Lesson 1:

God created you with a purpose in mind, and your life has meaning and significance.

Write a letter to yourself, reflecting on moments in your life where you felt a sense of purpose and significance. Describe those experiences and how they impacted you. Then, write about any moments when you felt unsure of your purpose or doubted your significance. Use this exercise to recognize the importance of purpose in your life.

Create a list of your strengths, passions, and unique qualities. Reflect on how these attributes might align with a greater purpose or contribute to the world around you. Write about how discovering and utilizing these strengths can enhance your sense of meaning and significance.

_____

_____

_____

_____

_____

_____

_____

_____

_____

_____

_____

_____

_____

_____

_____

_____

_____

_____

_____

_____

_____

_____

_____

_____

Think about someone you admire or look up to for their sense of purpose and significance in life. Write down the qualities and actions that make them stand out to you. Consider how you can incorporate some of those attributes into your own life to enhance your sense of purpose and significance.

Lesson 2:

Understanding and embracing your purpose is the foundation for a fulfilling and meaningful life.

Write a personal mission statement that articulates your purpose and values in life. Consider what you want to achieve, contribute, and be remembered for. Use this mission statement as a guiding principle in your decision-making and daily actions.

Take time to reflect on past experiences, both positive and challenging, that have shaped your understanding of purpose. Write about how these experiences have influenced your current perspective on life's meaning and the importance of embracing your purpose.

_____

_____

_____

_____

_____

_____

_____

_____

_____

_____

_____

_____

_____

_____

_____

_____

_____

_____

_____

_____

_____

_____

_____

_____

_____

_____

_____

Identify any limiting beliefs or self-doubt that may be hindering you from fully embracing your purpose. Write down positive affirmations and self-encouragement to counter these doubts. Keep these affirmations handy as reminders to stay focused on your purpose.

Lesson 3:

Seeking God's guidance and surrendering to His plan for your life will lead to a deeper sense of purpose and fulfillment.

Set aside time for prayer or meditation, seeking guidance from God about your purpose and life's direction. Write down any insights, thoughts, or feelings that come to you during this time of reflection.

Write a letter to God, expressing your willingness to surrender your plans and desires to His will. Share your hopes, dreams, and uncertainties, and ask for His guidance in aligning your life with His purpose.

_____

_____

_____

_____

_____

_____

_____

_____

_____

_____

_____

_____

_____

_____

_____

_____

_____

_____

_____

_____

_____

_____

_____

_____

Identify specific actions or habits you can incorporate into your daily life to stay connected to God and His guidance. Write down a plan for nurturing your spiritual relationship and staying open to His leading in your life.

Chapter 2:
You Are Not an Accident

Lesson 1:

Your existence is not a result of chance or coincidence; you are intentionally and purposefully created by God.

Write a letter to yourself, expressing gratitude for your existence and acknowledging that your life has purpose and meaning. Reflect on specific events or experiences that make you believe your creation is intentional and not accidental.

Research and study passages from religious texts or books that affirm the idea of intentional creation by a higher power. Write down verses or quotes that resonate with you and reinforce your belief in being purposefully created.

Talk to a friend or family member about their belief in intentional creation. Engage in a meaningful discussion about the evidence or experiences that support this belief. Write down the key points from your conversation and any insights gained.

_____

_____

_____

_____

_____

_____

_____

_____

_____

_____

_____

_____

_____

_____

_____

_____

_____

_____

_____

_____

_____

_____

_____

_____

_____

Lesson 2:

Accepting that you are not an accident empowers you to embrace your uniqueness and individuality.

Make a list of your unique qualities, talents, and strengths. Write about how each of these attributes sets you apart and contributes to the person you are today. Embrace and celebrate the aspects that make you unique.

Think about a time when you felt pressured to conform to societal norms or expectations. Write about how embracing your individuality in that situation could have empowered you to stay true to yourself.

_____

_____

_____

_____

_____

_____

_____

_____

_____

_____

_____

_____

_____

_____

_____

_____

_____

_____

_____

_____

_____

_____

_____

_____

Create a vision board that represents your individuality and uniqueness. Use images, quotes, and symbols that resonate with you and reflect who you are. Display the vision board in a prominent place as a reminder of your worth and individuality.

_____

_____

_____

_____

_____

_____

_____

_____

_____

_____

_____

_____

_____

_____

_____

_____

_____

_____

_____

_____

_____

_____

_____

_____

_____

Lesson 3:

Embracing your identity as a deliberate creation of God gives you a sense of belonging and worth.

Write a letter to God, expressing your feelings about being His deliberate creation. Thank Him for your life and acknowledge the sense of belonging and worth that comes from embracing this truth.

Consider the times when you may have felt inadequate or unworthy.
Write about how embracing your identity as a creation of God can
counter these feelings and boost your sense of worth.

_____
_____
_____
_____
_____
_____
_____
_____
_____
_____
_____
_____
_____
_____
_____
_____
_____
_____
_____
_____
_____
_____
_____
_____
_____
_____

Practice daily affirmations that reinforce your identity as a valued creation of God. Write down positive affirmations such as "I am intentionally created and valued by God" or "I am worthy of love and belonging." Repeat these affirmations daily to reinforce your sense of worth.

Chapter 3:
What Drives Your Life?

Lesson 1:

Everyone is driven by something, be it success, approval, material possessions, or other motivations.

Create a list of your top priorities and motivations in life. Write down the things that drive you, such as career success, financial security, personal achievements, or recognition from others. Reflect on how these motivations have influenced your decisions and actions.

Identify any external influences or societal expectations that drive your choices. Write about how these external factors may have influenced your values and priorities. Consider whether they align with your true desires and beliefs.

Take a moment to explore your emotions and feelings when you achieve or fail to achieve specific goals. Write about how your emotions are tied to your motivations and how they impact your overall sense of fulfillment and well-being.

Lesson 2:

Identifying the driving forces in your life is essential for understanding your priorities and making intentional choices.

Reflect on a recent decision you made and the factors that influenced it. Write about whether the motivations behind that decision align with your long-term goals and values. If they don't align, explore how you can make more intentional choices in the future.

Make a list of your core values and beliefs. Write about how these values guide your decision-making process and how they help you stay focused on what truly matters to you.

_____

_____

_____

_____

_____

_____

_____

_____

_____

_____

_____

_____

_____

_____

_____

_____

_____

_____

_____

_____

_____

_____

_____

_____

_____

_____

_____

_____

_____

_____

Create a "Values Alignment Chart." List your top priorities and motivations on one side and your core values on the other side. Evaluate how well each motivation aligns with your values. Use this chart as a tool to guide your choices and prioritize what truly matters to you.

_____

_____

_____

_____

_____

_____

_____

_____

_____

_____

_____

_____

_____

_____

_____

_____

_____

_____

_____

_____

_____

_____

_____

_____

Lesson 3:

Aligning your life with God's purposes and values will lead to greater fulfillment and harmony.

Write a letter to God, expressing your desire to align your life with His purposes and values. Share your willingness to surrender your motivations to Him and seek His guidance in making decisions that honor His plan for your life.

Identify areas of your life where you feel disconnected from God's purposes and values. Write about the changes you can make to re-align these areas with His will. Consider how these changes might lead to a greater sense of fulfillment and harmony.

_____

_____

_____

_____

_____

_____

_____

_____

_____

_____

_____

_____

_____

_____

_____

_____

_____

_____

_____

_____

_____

_____

_____

_____

_____

Practice daily prayer or meditation to seek God's guidance in making choices and decisions. Write down any insights or messages you receive during these moments of reflection. Use these insights as a compass to align your life with God's purposes and values.

Chapter 4:
Made to Last Forever

Lesson 1:

Your life on Earth is just the beginning; eternity awaits beyond this temporary existence

Write a reflection on the concept of eternity and how it shapes your perspective on life and the world around you. Consider how embracing the idea of an eternal existence influences the way you prioritize and value your time on Earth.

Imagine yourself in an eternal state, looking back at your life on Earth. Write a letter to your present self, sharing what you hope to accomplish and experience during your temporary existence. Use this letter as a reminder to make the most of your time on Earth.

Research different religious or philosophical beliefs about the after-life and eternity. Write about how these perspectives resonate with you and how they may influence the way you live your life in the present.

_____

_____

_____

_____

_____

_____

_____

_____

_____

_____

_____

_____

_____

_____

_____

_____

_____

_____

_____

_____

_____

_____

_____

_____

_____

_____

_____

_____

Lesson 2:

Preparing for eternity involves living a life of love, service, and devotion to God and others

List specific acts of love and service you can perform for others in your daily life. Write about how incorporating these actions into your routine can bring a sense of purpose and fulfillment to your existence.

Take time to reflect on your relationship with God and your level of devotion to Him. Write a prayer or expression of commitment, vowing to deepen your devotion and seek His guidance in living a life of love and service.

_____

_____

_____

_____

_____

_____

_____

_____

_____

_____

_____

_____

_____

_____

_____

_____

_____

_____

_____

_____

_____

_____

_____

_____

Identify any barriers or distractions that hinder you from living a life of love and service. Write about strategies you can implement to overcome these obstacles and make a more significant impact on the lives of others.

Lesson 3:

Your actions and choices on Earth have eternal consequences, so investing in what matters most will bring lasting rewards.

Create a "Prioritization Grid" that lists various aspects of your life, such as family, career, hobbies, and personal growth. Rank these aspects based on their potential for eternal impact. Write about the insights gained from this exercise and how it influences your future choices.

_____

_____

_____

_____

_____

_____

_____

_____

_____

_____

_____

_____

_____

_____

_____

_____

_____

_____

_____

_____

_____

_____

_____

_____

Think about a time when you made a decision based on short-term benefits, neglecting the potential long-term consequences. Write about the lessons you learned from that experience and how you can approach similar situations differently in the future.

Write a letter to your future self, describing the legacy you hope to leave behind and the impact you want to have on future generations. Use this letter as a motivation to invest in what truly matters and make choices that align with your long-term vision.

Chapter 5:
Seeing Life from God's View

Lesson 1:

Seeing life from God's perspective enables you to understand the bigger picture and divine purposes at work.

Spend time in nature or a quiet place where you can reflect on the wonders of creation. Write about the feelings and insights that arise from observing God's handiwork. Consider how this experience helps you see life from a broader, more awe-inspiring perspective.

Choose a significant event or challenging situation from your life. Write about how seeing this event from God's viewpoint might change your understanding of its purpose and impact. Explore the idea of trusting in His larger plan.

Study stories of faith and resilience from religious texts or other sources. Write about the lessons you can learn from these stories and how they inspire you to view your own life with a deeper sense of purpose and meaning.

_____

_____

_____

_____

_____

_____

_____

_____

_____

_____

_____

_____

_____

_____

_____

_____

_____

_____

_____

_____

_____

_____

_____

_____

Lesson 2:

Seeking God's guidance through prayer and studying His Word allows you to discern His will for your life.

Create a prayer journal to record your conversations with God.
Write about your hopes, fears, and desires, and then reflect on how
you sense His guidance or presence in your life. Use this journal to
track any patterns or recurring themes in His responses.

Choose a meaningful passage from a religious text that relates to a current decision or dilemma in your life. Write about how studying this passage helps you discern God's will and make choices in alignment with His guidance.

_____

_____

_____

_____

_____

_____

_____

_____

_____

_____

_____

_____

_____

_____

_____

_____

_____

_____

_____

_____

_____

_____

_____

_____

_____

Write a letter to God, asking for clarity and understanding regarding a specific aspect of your life. Describe the feelings or thoughts that arise during this prayer, and reflect on any insights or guidance you receive.

Lesson 3:

Embracing God's view of life helps you navigate challenges with faith and hope, trusting that He is in control.

Identify a recent challenge or hardship you faced. Write about how embracing God's perspective on the situation changes your feelings and outlook. Explore how faith and hope in His plan help you cope with difficulties.

_____

_____

_____

_____

_____

_____

_____

_____

_____

_____

_____

_____

_____

_____

_____

_____

_____

_____

_____

_____

_____

_____

_____

_____

_____

_____

_____

_____

_____

Create a gratitude journal to document the blessings and miracles you encounter daily. Write about how these experiences reinforce your trust in God's control and bring a sense of peace and assurance.

_____

_____

_____

_____

_____

_____

_____

_____

_____

_____

_____

_____

_____

_____

_____

_____

_____

_____

_____

_____

_____

_____

_____

_____

_____

Study scriptures or passages that encourage trust in God's providence and control over life's circumstances. Write down affirmations or verses that resonate with you, and keep them as reminders to maintain faith and hope during challenging times.

Chapter 6:
Life Is a Temporary Assignment

Lesson 1:

Your time on Earth is temporary, and viewing life as an assignment helps you focus on fulfilling your God-given purpose.

Write a letter to your future self, imagining yourself at the end of your life reflecting on how you lived your temporary assignment. Describe the legacy you hope to leave behind and the impact you want to make on others and the world.

Create a "Life Assignment Plan" that outlines specific goals and actions you want to accomplish during your time on Earth. Write about how each goal aligns with your God-given purpose and how achieving them contributes to your life assignment.

_____

_____

_____

_____

_____

_____

_____

_____

_____

_____

_____

_____

_____

_____

_____

_____

_____

_____

_____

_____

_____

_____

_____

_____

_____

Identify any distractions or time-wasting activities in your daily life. Write about how detaching from these distractions can help you stay focused on your life assignment and make the most of your time.

_____

_____

_____

_____

_____

_____

_____

_____

_____

_____

_____

_____

_____

_____

_____

_____

_____

_____

_____

_____

_____

_____

_____

_____

_____

_____

_____

_____

_____

Lesson 2:

Detaching from material possessions and temporal pursuits allows you to invest in what truly matters for eternity.

Take inventory of your material possessions and evaluate their significance in your life. Write about the items that truly hold value beyond their temporal nature and those that you can detach from to prioritize what truly matters.

Reflect on the activities and pursuits that consume much of your time and energy. Write about how these pursuits align with your eternal purpose and how you can reorient your focus to invest more in what truly matters.

_____

_____

_____

_____

_____

_____

_____

_____

_____

_____

_____

_____

_____

_____

_____

_____

_____

_____

_____

_____

_____

_____

_____

_____

_____

Create a "Simplicity and Purpose" chart. On one side, list material possessions and temporal pursuits that add complexity to your life. On the other side, list activities and practices that align with your God-given purpose. Write about how you can simplify your life by detaching from the former and investing in the latter.

Lesson 3:

Embracing the temporariness of life motivates you to live with intention and purpose, making the most of the time you have.

Write a personal mission statement that captures the essence of your life's purpose and how you want to make the most of your time on Earth. Use this mission statement as a guiding principle for your daily decisions and actions.

Identify your top three priorities in life and write about how you can align your daily activities with these priorities. Consider how living with intention and purpose in these areas can lead to greater fulfillment and impact.

_____

_____

_____

_____

_____

_____

_____

_____

_____

_____

_____

_____

_____

_____

_____

_____

_____

_____

_____

_____

_____

_____

_____

_____

_____

_____

Imagine yourself at the end of your life, looking back on the time you spent on Earth. Write a journal entry about the accomplishments, relationships, and experiences you hope to cherish as you embrace the temporariness of life.

Chapter 7:
The Reason for Everything

Lesson 1:

Everything in the universe was created for God's pleasure and glory.

Reflect on the beauty and intricacies of nature around you. Write about how these elements showcase God's creativity and bring Him pleasure and glory. Consider how you can honor God by appreciating and caring for His creation.

Study religious texts or writings that emphasize God's pleasure and glory in His creation. Write down verses or quotes that resonate with you and inspire a deeper understanding of His purposes.

_____

_____

_____

_____

_____

_____

_____

_____

_____

_____

_____

_____

_____

_____

_____

_____

_____

_____

_____

_____

_____

_____

_____

_____

_____

_____

Write a prayer expressing gratitude for being part of God's creation and acknowledging your desire to live in a way that brings Him pleasure and glory. Use this prayer as a daily reminder of your purpose.

Lesson 2:

Living for God's glory means seeking to honor Him in all areas of life, including relationships, work, and personal growth.

Create a "Glory Checklist" that includes different aspects of your life, such as family, career, hobbies, and self-improvement. Write about how you can honor God in each area and the actions you can take to align your life with His glory.

Identify any areas of your life where you feel disconnected from God's glory. Write about the steps you can take to realign these areas with His will and bring Him honor through your actions.

_____

_____

_____

_____

_____

_____

_____

_____

_____

_____

_____

_____

_____

_____

_____

_____

_____

_____

_____

_____

_____

_____

_____

_____

_____

_____

_____

Think about a recent interaction with someone in your life, and write about how you can show God's love and grace in that relationship. Consider ways to demonstrate compassion, forgiveness, and understanding as you seek to honor God in your connections.

Lesson 3:

Prioritizing God's pleasure over self-gratification leads to a life of greater meaning and significance.

Examine your daily habits and routines. Write about which activities are driven by self-gratification and which ones align with honoring God. Consider how you can adjust your daily choices to prioritize His pleasure over personal desires.

Write a "Gratitude Journal" to document the moments when you chose to honor God's pleasure over self-gratification. Write about the impact of these choices on your overall sense of meaning and significance.

_____

_____

_____

_____

_____

_____

_____

_____

_____

_____

_____

_____

_____

_____

_____

_____

_____

_____

_____

_____

_____

_____

_____

_____

Identify any personal goals or aspirations that are primarily focused on self-gratification. Write about how you can reshape these goals to align with God's purposes and how doing so can lead to a more meaningful and purposeful life.

Made in United States
Cleveland, OH
22 October 2024

10253479R00049